Finding Comfort After the Storm
A Parent's Journal to Healing After Their Child's Trauma

Lindsay K. Krebs, MS Ed/CAS

Copyright © 2020 Lindsay K. Krebs
All Rights Reserved
ISBN – 13: 9781661366759

All rights reserved. No part of this publication may be reproduced or distributed in any form or by any means, including photocopying, without prior permission of the publisher.

If your child has endured some form of trauma (sexual abuse, physical abuse, emotional abuse, etc.) it is very common for parents and caregivers to go through an emotional turmoil following such events. You may feel guilt, anger, sadness, anxiety, and the list goes on. What is extremely important to understand, is that unless you were the actual perpetrator of this abuse, it is NOT your fault.

As parents and caregivers, you do all you can to love and protect your children from harm. Unfortunately, you cannot be everywhere at all times and, sadly, sometimes bad things do happen that are not within your control. Following the abuse of your child, it is vital to obtain support for your child, such a therapy, to help them work through their trauma. However, you too, as their parent or caregiver have also gone through this trauma with them. If you do not work on your own emotions and fall apart, you will be of little help to them in their recovery. Therefore, it is of the utmost importance to take care of YOU as well!

Please work hard to get your feelings out, in one way or another, as this is extremely important as you begin to heal from the trauma which has touched your family. Journaling is a very good place to begin to express your emotions. My sincere hope is that this journal will help to guide you through your healing process and to get your feelings out, whatever they may be.

You have every right to feel the way that you do, so please go ahead and use this journal as an outlet to get angry if you need to and to vent all of your feelings onto these pages. Leave no drop of emotion unwritten, simply GET IT OUT! However, if you feel that journaling is not helping you with all of the emotions you are feeling, perhaps you may want to consider obtaining therapy for yourself as well. There is NO shame in doing so. Remember, your child needs support following trauma, but so do his or her parents and caregivers. You make the decisions regarding your path to healing; the important part is not to forget yourself throughout this process.

The road a family walks, following a trauma, is far from easy. Trauma has been known to both pull families together, as well as to pull them apart. Keeping your feelings inside, where they build up until you very likely do or say something you may regret, will only increase the likelihood that your family will continue to suffer longer after the trauma.

If you have a significant other who has endured this trauma with you, perhaps you may want to consider both having a copy of this journal to get your feelings out. After doing so, having a daily, or at least weekly, discussion about what you have written regarding your feelings could be extremely vital to your family's healing process. These discussions will most likely not be easy at first, but in doing so, they will help open up the line of communication and help you to heal together.

Following a trauma such as this, it is of the utmost importance to also lean on your close family and friends. You certainly do not have to broadcast what has happened, as it is your choice who to disclose the trauma to and allow into your, "Inner circle." Leaning on select friends and family members whom you trust and can confide in, can be extremely helpful throughout the healing process. Even if they are simply a shoulder to cry on when your emotions are at their peak, you need that.

Please do not try to, "Go it alone." Feeling that you are alone throughout the trauma, will in no way help your healing process. In addition to journaling, therapy, friends, and family, there are also support groups on social media for different forms of trauma. Certainly, if you are able to locate a support group in your area, regarding the trauma your family has sustained, please consider attending. Support groups, either in-person or on social media, can be a wonderful tool to openly communicate with others who may have endured something similar, and will likely have a much better understanding of what your family has gone through.

I wish you the best in your healing process and am happy you have taken a great step by utilizing this journal. I very much hope that it can be a helpful tool for you, and help you to better navigate through the flood of emotions you are now feeling.

Much love,
Lindsay K. Krebs

My scars tell
a story. They are a
reminder of times
when life tried
to break me,
but failed.

~ Steve Maraboli

The first section of your journal is to help you address areas of your life that may be of immediate concern. These are things that you perhaps may not have considered, given the state of emotional turmoil you and your family have likely been experiencing since your child's trauma occurred. Please use these pages a reference to help guide you through difficult times as they arise throughout the healing process with your family. The words you have written on these pages can very much help guide you through emotional peaks as they come and go.

Date: _____

How are you feeling right now about the trauma that your child and your family have endured?

_____
_____
_____
_____
_____
_____
_____
_____
_____
_____
_____
_____
_____
_____
_____
_____
_____
_____
_____
_____
_____
_____
_____
_____

Life shrinks or expands in proportion to one's courage.

~ Anais Nin

Date: _____

How has your life changed since this trauma?

_____
_____
_____
_____
_____
_____
_____
_____
_____
_____
_____
_____
_____
_____
_____
_____
_____
_____
_____
_____
_____
_____
_____
_____

Do not let the behavior of others destroy your inner peace.

~ Dalai Lama

Date: _____

How has this trauma impacted your child?

_____
_____
_____
_____
_____
_____
_____
_____
_____
_____
_____
_____
_____
_____
_____
_____
_____
_____
_____
_____
_____
_____
_____
_____
_____
_____

You think you're walking through the darkness, not realizing you are the light for those walking beside you.

~ Stacie Martin

Date: _____

How has this trauma impacted you, specifically?

_____
_____
_____
_____
_____
_____
_____
_____
_____
_____
_____
_____
_____
_____
_____
_____
_____
_____
_____
_____
_____
_____
_____
_____
_____
_____
_____
_____
_____
_____

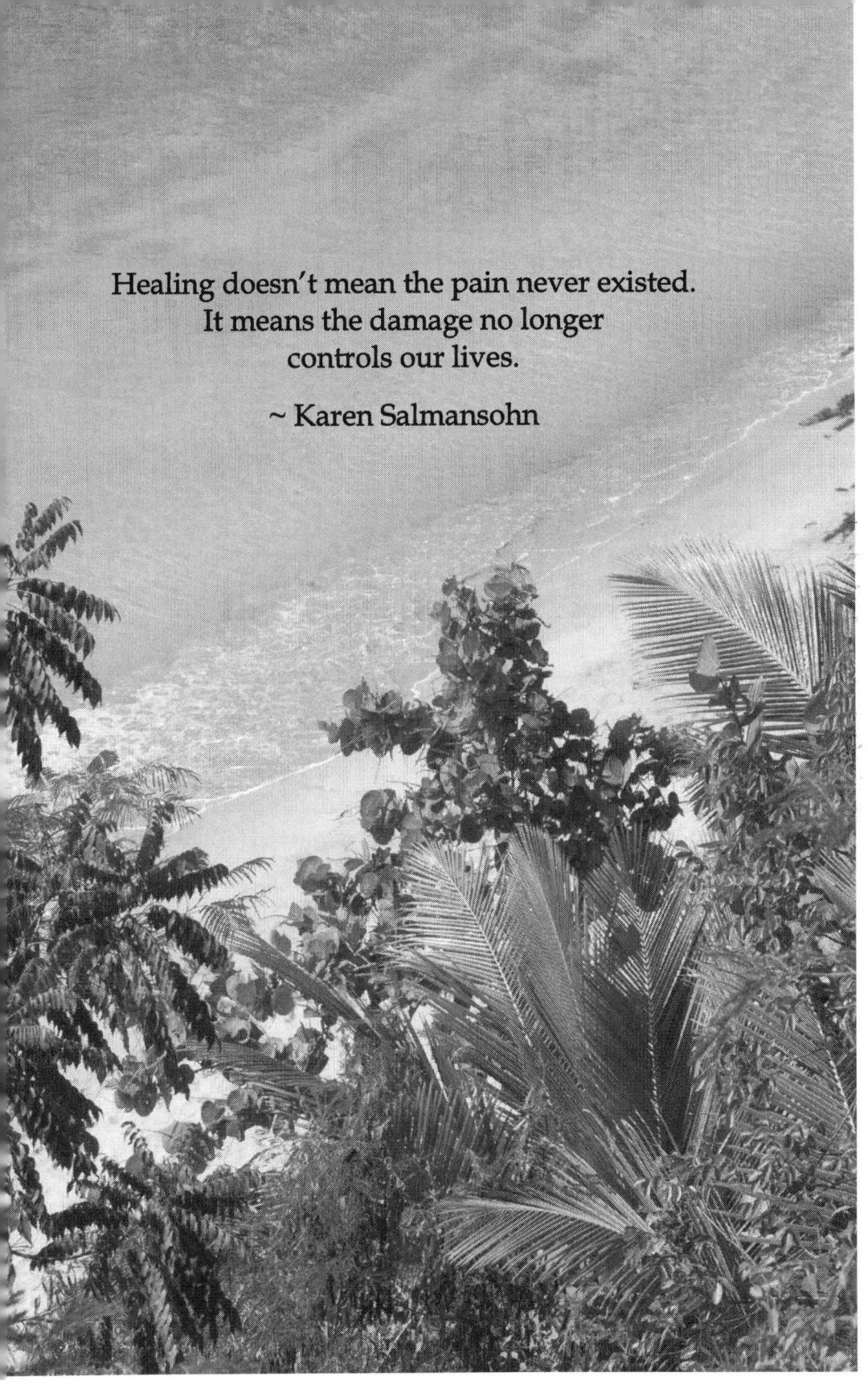

Healing doesn't mean the pain never existed.
It means the damage no longer
controls our lives.

~ Karen Salmansohn

Date: _____

How has this trauma impacted your relationships with others?

_____
_____
_____
_____
_____
_____
_____
_____
_____
_____
_____
_____
_____
_____
_____
_____
_____
_____
_____
_____
_____
_____
_____
_____

We remember the people who show up
in our darkest hours.

~ Shauna L. Hoey

Date: _____

What have you done to help your child following his or her trauma?

_____

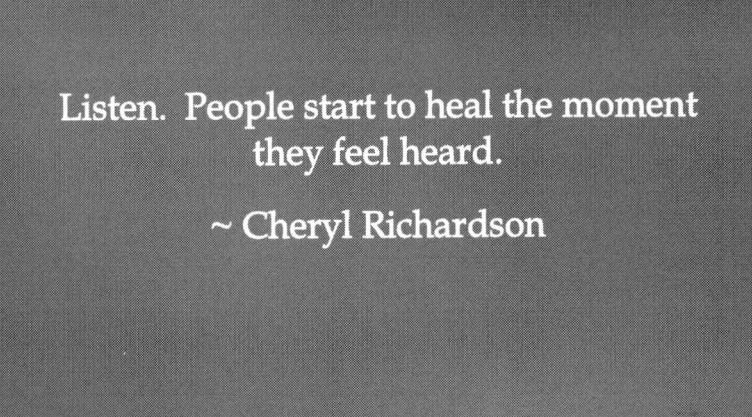

Listen. People start to heal the moment they feel heard.

~ Cheryl Richardson

Date: _____

What have you done to help YOURSELF following this trauma?

_____
_____
_____
_____
_____
_____
_____
_____
_____
_____
_____
_____
_____
_____
_____
_____
_____
_____
_____
_____
_____
_____
_____
_____
_____
_____
_____
_____

Healing doesn't just take a little time; it also takes commitment to get started and to complete the process.

~ Sereda Aleta Dailey

Date: _____

If you have not focused on taking care of yourself following this trauma, what could you do for YOU? Self-care isn't selfish, it's necessary!

_____
_____
_____
_____
_____
_____
_____
_____
_____
_____
_____
_____
_____
_____
_____
_____
_____
_____
_____
_____
_____
_____
_____
_____
_____

It does not matter how slowly you go as long as you do not stop.

~ Confucius

Date: _____

What support do you have in place for yourself?
Who can you go to when your emotions
are at their peak?

_____
_____
_____
_____
_____
_____
_____
_____
_____
_____
_____
_____
_____
_____
_____
_____
_____
_____
_____
_____
_____
_____
_____
_____
_____

We don't heal in isolation, but in community.

~ S. Kelley Harrell

Date: _____

What can you do to work on strengthening any relationships that may now be, "Rocky," following this trauma?

___

Take all the time you need to heal emotionally. Heal at your own pace, step by step, day by day.

~ Karen Salmansohn

Date: _____

It is so very important not to let your emotions consume you following a family trauma. What could you do to help yourself have a more positive outlook on life, for the good for both you and your family?

_____
_____
_____
_____
_____
_____
_____
_____
_____
_____
_____
_____
_____
_____
_____
_____
_____
_____
_____
_____
_____
_____
_____
_____
_____

Start where you are. Use what you have.
Do what you can.

−Arthur Ashe

Date: _____

Sadly, sometimes we find that others are not very supportive following a trauma, which only seems to add unnecessary anguish. Are there perhaps any, "Toxic," individuals in your life following the trauma that you might want to cut ties with to heal? This is not easy, but sometimes it's necessary.

_____
_____
_____
_____
_____
_____
_____
_____
_____
_____
_____
_____
_____
_____
_____
_____
_____
_____
_____
_____
_____
_____
_____

Happiness is not something readymade.
It comes from your own actions.

~ Dalai Lama

Date: _____

How are you feeling now that you have had the opportunity to really consider your emotions and your life in general, following this trauma?

_____
_____
_____
_____
_____
_____
_____
_____
_____
_____
_____
_____
_____
_____
_____
_____
_____
_____
_____
_____
_____
_____
_____
_____
_____

The second section of your journal is to provide you with a daily outlet for your feelings. These pages will allow you more freedom to write whatever comes to mind and is weighing on your heart on that particular day. To aid in your healing process, you are encouraged to continue to write in your journal, as an outlet for your emotions as they continue to
ebb and flow.

Always remember that you are not alone. The first section of this journal can be used as a good reference to help guide you throughout the healing process.

Date: _____

What is weighing on your heart today?

_____
_____
_____
_____
_____
_____
_____
_____
_____
_____
_____
_____
_____
_____
_____
_____
_____
_____
_____
_____
_____
_____
_____
_____
_____
_____
_____
_____

Date: _____

What is weighing on your heart today?

_____
_____
_____
_____
_____
_____
_____
_____
_____
_____
_____
_____
_____
_____
_____
_____
_____
_____
_____
_____
_____
_____
_____
_____
_____
_____
_____
_____
_____
_____

Date: _____

What is weighing on your heart today?

Date: _____

What is weighing on your heart today?

_____
_____
_____
_____
_____
_____
_____
_____
_____
_____
_____
_____
_____
_____
_____
_____
_____
_____
_____
_____
_____
_____
_____
_____
_____
_____
_____
_____
_____
_____
_____

Date: _____

What is weighing on your heart today?

_____
_____
_____
_____
_____
_____
_____
_____
_____
_____
_____
_____
_____
_____
_____
_____
_____
_____
_____
_____
_____
_____
_____
_____
_____
_____

Nobody can bring you peace but yourself.

~ Ralph Waldo Emerson

Date: _____

What is weighing on your heart today?

_____
_____
_____
_____
_____
_____
_____
_____
_____
_____
_____
_____
_____
_____
_____
_____
_____
_____
_____
_____
_____
_____
_____
_____

Date: _____

What is weighing on your heart today?

_____
_____
_____
_____
_____
_____
_____
_____
_____
_____
_____
_____
_____
_____
_____
_____
_____
_____
_____
_____
_____
_____
_____
_____
_____
_____
_____
_____
_____
_____

Date: _____

What is weighing on your heart today?

_____
_____
_____
_____
_____
_____
_____
_____
_____
_____
_____
_____
_____
_____
_____
_____
_____
_____
_____
_____
_____
_____
_____
_____
_____

Date: _____

What is weighing on your heart today?

Date: _____

What is weighing on your heart today?

You will find peace not by trying to escape your problems, but by confronting them courageously. You will find peace not in denial, but in victory.

~ J. Donald Walters

Date: _____

What is weighing on your heart today?

_____
_____
_____
_____
_____
_____
_____
_____
_____
_____
_____
_____
_____
_____
_____
_____
_____
_____
_____
_____
_____
_____
_____
_____
_____
_____
_____

Date: _____

What is weighing on your heart today?

_____
_____
_____
_____
_____
_____
_____
_____
_____
_____
_____
_____
_____
_____
_____
_____
_____
_____
_____
_____
_____
_____
_____
_____
_____
_____
_____
_____
_____
_____

Date: _____

What is weighing on your heart today?

_____
_____
_____
_____
_____
_____
_____
_____
_____
_____
_____
_____
_____
_____
_____
_____
_____
_____
_____
_____
_____
_____
_____
_____
_____
_____
_____
_____

Date: _____

What is weighing on your heart today?

_____
_____
_____
_____
_____
_____
_____
_____
_____
_____
_____
_____
_____
_____
_____
_____
_____
_____
_____
_____
_____
_____
_____
_____
_____
_____
_____
_____
_____
_____

Date: _____

What is weighing on your heart today?

_____

Peace is a daily, a weekly, a monthly process, gradually changing opinions, slowly eroding old barriers, quietly building new structures.

~ John F. Kennedy

Date: _____

What is weighing on your heart today?

_____
_____
_____
_____
_____
_____
_____
_____
_____
_____
_____
_____
_____
_____
_____
_____
_____
_____
_____
_____
_____
_____
_____
_____
_____
_____
_____

Date: _____

What is weighing on your heart today?

_____
_____
_____
_____
_____
_____
_____
_____
_____
_____
_____
_____
_____
_____
_____
_____
_____
_____
_____
_____
_____
_____
_____
_____
_____
_____
_____
_____
_____
_____
_____

Date: _____

What is weighing on your heart today?

_____
_____
_____
_____
_____
_____
_____
_____
_____
_____
_____
_____
_____
_____
_____
_____
_____
_____
_____
_____
_____
_____
_____
_____
_____
_____
_____

Date: _____

What is weighing on your heart today?

_____
_____
_____
_____
_____
_____
_____
_____
_____
_____
_____
_____
_____
_____
_____
_____
_____
_____
_____
_____
_____
_____
_____
_____
_____
_____
_____
_____
_____
_____

Date: _____

What is weighing on your heart today?

_____
_____
_____
_____
_____
_____
_____
_____
_____
_____
_____
_____
_____
_____
_____
_____
_____
_____
_____
_____
_____
_____
_____
_____
_____
_____

Keep your face towards
the sunshine, and
shadows will fall
behind you.

~ Walt Whitman

Date: _____

What is weighing on your heart today?

_____
_____
_____
_____
_____
_____
_____
_____
_____
_____
_____
_____
_____
_____
_____
_____
_____
_____
_____
_____
_____
_____
_____
_____
_____
_____

Date: _____

What is weighing on your heart today?

_____
_____
_____
_____
_____
_____
_____
_____
_____
_____
_____
_____
_____
_____
_____
_____
_____
_____
_____
_____
_____
_____
_____
_____
_____
_____
_____
_____
_____
_____

Date: _____

What is weighing on your heart today?

_____
_____
_____
_____
_____
_____
_____
_____
_____
_____
_____
_____
_____
_____
_____
_____
_____
_____
_____
_____
_____
_____
_____
_____
_____
_____
_____
_____
_____

Date: _____

What is weighing on your heart today?

_____
_____
_____
_____
_____
_____
_____
_____
_____
_____
_____
_____
_____
_____
_____
_____
_____
_____
_____
_____
_____
_____
_____
_____
_____
_____
_____
_____
_____

Date: _____

What is weighing on your heart today?

_____
_____
_____
_____
_____
_____
_____
_____
_____
_____
_____
_____
_____
_____
_____
_____
_____
_____
_____
_____
_____
_____
_____
_____
_____
_____
_____
_____

Believe you can and you're halfway there.

~ Theodore Roosevelt

Date: _____

What is weighing on your heart today?

_____
_____
_____
_____
_____
_____
_____
_____
_____
_____
_____
_____
_____
_____
_____
_____
_____
_____
_____
_____
_____
_____
_____
_____
_____
_____

Date: _____

What is weighing on your heart today?

_____
_____
_____
_____
_____
_____
_____
_____
_____
_____
_____
_____
_____
_____
_____
_____
_____
_____
_____
_____
_____
_____
_____
_____
_____
_____
_____
_____
_____
_____

Date: _____

What is weighing on your heart today?

_____
_____
_____
_____
_____
_____
_____
_____
_____
_____
_____
_____
_____
_____
_____
_____
_____
_____
_____
_____
_____
_____
_____
_____
_____
_____
_____
_____

Date: _____

What is weighing on your heart today?

_____
_____
_____
_____
_____
_____
_____
_____
_____
_____
_____
_____
_____
_____
_____
_____
_____
_____
_____
_____
_____
_____
_____
_____
_____
_____
_____
_____
_____
_____
_____

Date: _____

What is weighing on your heart today?

_____
_____
_____
_____
_____
_____
_____
_____
_____
_____
_____
_____
_____
_____
_____
_____
_____
_____
_____
_____
_____
_____
_____
_____
_____
_____

When everything seems to be going against you, remember that the airplane takes off against the wind, not with it.

~ Henry Ford

Date: _____

What is weighing on your heart today?

_____
_____
_____
_____
_____
_____
_____
_____
_____
_____
_____
_____
_____
_____
_____
_____
_____
_____
_____
_____
_____
_____
_____
_____
_____
_____
_____
_____
_____

Date: _____

What is weighing on your heart today?

Date: _____

What is weighing on your heart today?

_____
_____
_____
_____
_____
_____
_____
_____
_____
_____
_____
_____
_____
_____
_____
_____
_____
_____
_____
_____
_____
_____
_____
_____
_____
_____
_____

Date: _____

What is weighing on your heart today?

_____
_____
_____
_____
_____
_____
_____
_____
_____
_____
_____
_____
_____
_____
_____
_____
_____
_____
_____
_____
_____
_____
_____
_____
_____
_____
_____
_____
_____
_____

Date: _____

What is weighing on your heart today?

_____
_____
_____
_____
_____
_____
_____
_____
_____
_____
_____
_____
_____
_____
_____
_____
_____
_____
_____
_____
_____
_____
_____
_____
_____
_____
_____
_____
_____
_____

Everyone has the potential to live a fulfilling life. The difference lies in how we look at things.

~ Vishal Pandey

Date: _____

What is weighing on your heart today?

Date: _____

What is weighing on your heart today?

_____
_____
_____
_____
_____
_____
_____
_____
_____
_____
_____
_____
_____
_____
_____
_____
_____
_____
_____
_____
_____
_____
_____
_____
_____
_____
_____
_____
_____

Date: _____

What is weighing on your heart today?

_____
_____
_____
_____
_____
_____
_____
_____
_____
_____
_____
_____
_____
_____
_____
_____
_____
_____
_____
_____
_____
_____
_____
_____
_____
_____
_____

Date: _____

What is weighing on your heart today?

_____
_____
_____
_____
_____
_____
_____
_____
_____
_____
_____
_____
_____
_____
_____
_____
_____
_____
_____
_____
_____
_____
_____
_____
_____
_____
_____
_____

Date: _____

What is weighing on your heart today?

You can't fall if you don't climb. But there's no joy in living your whole life on the ground.

~ Unknown

Date: _____

What is weighing on your heart today?

_____
_____
_____
_____
_____
_____
_____
_____
_____
_____
_____
_____
_____
_____
_____
_____
_____
_____
_____
_____
_____
_____
_____
_____
_____
_____
_____
_____
_____
_____

Date: _____

What is weighing on your heart today?

_____
_____
_____
_____
_____
_____
_____
_____
_____
_____
_____
_____
_____
_____
_____
_____
_____
_____
_____
_____
_____
_____
_____
_____
_____
_____
_____
_____
_____
_____
_____

Date: _____

What is weighing on your heart today?

_____
_____
_____
_____
_____
_____
_____
_____
_____
_____
_____
_____
_____
_____
_____
_____
_____
_____
_____
_____
_____
_____
_____
_____
_____
_____
_____
_____
_____

Date: _____

What is weighing on your heart today?

_____
_____
_____
_____
_____
_____
_____
_____
_____
_____
_____
_____
_____
_____
_____
_____
_____
_____
_____
_____
_____
_____
_____
_____
_____
_____
_____
_____
_____
_____
_____
_____

Date: _____

What is weighing on your heart today?

_____
_____
_____
_____
_____
_____
_____
_____
_____
_____
_____
_____
_____
_____
_____
_____
_____
_____
_____
_____
_____
_____
_____
_____
_____
_____

Made in the USA
Middletown, DE
08 February 2020